BATTLE ROYALE

KOUSHUN TAKAMI & MASAYUKI TAGUCHI

ALSO AVAILABLE FROM TOKYOPOP®

MANGA

IACK//LEGEND OF THE TWILIGHT*
@LARGE (December 2003)
NGELIC LAYER*
ABY BIRTH*
ATTLE ROYALE*
RAIN POWERED*
RIGADOON*
ARDCAPTOR SAKURA
ARDCAPTOR SAKURA: MASTER OF THE CLOW*
HOBITS*
HRONICLES OF THE CURSED SWORD
LAMP SCHOOL DETECTIVES*
LOVER
ONFIDENTIAL CONFESSIONS*
ORRECTOR YUI
OWBOY BEBOP*
OWBOY BEBOP: SHOOTING STAR*
YBORG 009*
EMON DIARY
IGIMON*
RAGON HUNTER
RAGON KNIGHTS*
UKLYON: CLAMP SCHOOL DEFENDERS*
RICA SAKURAZAWA*
AKE*
LCL*
ORBIDDEN DANCE*
ATE KEEPERS*
GUNDAM*
RAVITATION*
TO*
UNDAM WING
UNDAM WING: BATTLEFIELD OF PACIFISTS
UNDAM WING: ENDLESS WALTZ*
UNDAM WING: THE LAST OUTPOST*
APPY MANIA*
ARLEM BEAT
.N.V.U.
NITIAL D*
SLAND
ING: KING OF BANDITS*
ULINE
ARE KANO*
INDAICHI CASE FILES, THE*
ING OF HELL
ODOCHA: SANA'S STAGE*
OVE HINA*
UPIN III*
AGIC KNIGHT RAYEARTH*
MAGIC KNIGHT RAYEARTH II* (COMING SOON)
MAN OF MANY FACES*
MARMALADE BOY*
MARS*
MIRACLE GIRLS
MIYUKI-CHAN IN WONDERLAND*
MONSTERS, INC.
PARADISE KISS*
PARASYTE
PEACH GIRL
PEACH GIRL: CHANGE OF HEART*
PET SHOP OF HORRORS*
PLANET LADDER*
PLANETES*
PRIEST
RAGNAROK
RAVE MASTER*
REALITY CHECK
REBIRTH
REBOUND*
RISING STARS OF MANGA
SABER MARIONETTE J*
SAILOR MOON
SAINT TAIL
SAMURAI DEEPER KYO*
SAMURAI GIRL: REAL BOUT HIGH SCHOOL*
SCRYED*
SHAOLIN SISTERS*
SHIRAHIME-SYO: SNOW GODDESS TALES* (Dec. 2003)
SHUTTERBOX
SORCERER HUNTERS
THE SKULL MAN*
THE VISION OF ESCAFLOWNE*
TOKYO MEW MEW*
UNDER THE GLASS MOON
VAMPIRE GAME*
WILD ACT*
WISH*
WORLD OF HARTZ
X-DAY*
ZODIAC P.I. *

For more information visit www.TOKYOPOP.com

100% AUTHENTIC MANGA

*INDICATES 100% AUTHENTIC MANGA (RIGHT-TO-LEFT FORMAT)

CINE-MANGA™

ARDCAPTORS
ACKIE CHAN ADVENTURES
IMMY NEUTRON
IM POSSIBLE
IZZIE MCGUIRE
OWER RANGERS: NINJA STORM
PONGEBOB SQUAREPANTS
PY KIDS 2

NOVELS

ARMA CLUB (April 2004)
AILOR MOON

TOKYOPOP KIDS

STRAY SHEEP

ART BOOKS

CARDCAPTOR SAKURA*
MAGIC KNIGHT RAYEARTH*

ANIME GUIDES

COWBOY BEBOP ANIME GUIDES
GUNDAM TECHNICAL MANUALS
SAILOR MOON SCOUT GUIDES

090503

BATTLE ROYALE

BY

KOUSHUN TAKAMI & MASAYUKI TAGUCHI

VOL. 1

LOS ANGELES • LONDON • TOKYO • HAMBURG

Translator - Takako Maeda & Tomo Iwo
English Adaptation - Keith Giffen
Retouch and Lettering - Towfic Kassis & Anna Kernbaum
Cover Layout - Gary Shum
Graphic Designer - Mark Paniccia

Editor - Mark Paniccia
Digital Imaging Manager - Chris Buford
Pre-Press Manager - Antonio DePietro
Production Managers - Jennifer Miller, Mutsumi Miyazaki
Art Director - Matt Alford
Managing Editor - Jill Freshney
VP of Production - Ron Klamert
President & C.O.O. - John Parker
Publisher & C.E.O. - Stuart Levy

E-mail: info@TOKYOPOP.com
Come visit us online at www.TOKYOPOP.com

A TOKYOPOP® Manga

TOKYOPOP Inc.
5900 Wilshire Blvd. Suite 2000
Los Angeles, CA 90036

Battle Royale Vol. 1

BATTLE ROYALE Vol. 1 © 2000 Koushun Takami/Masayuki Taguchi. All rights reserved.
First published in Japan in 2000 by Akita Publishing Co,.Ltd. Tokyo
English translation rights arranged through Akita Publishing Co,. Ltd.

English text copyright ©2004 TOKYOPOP Inc.

All rights reserved. No portion of this book may be reproduced or transmitted in any form or by any means without written permission from the copyright holders. This manga is a work of fiction. Any resemblance to actual events or locales or persons, living or dead, is entirely coincidental.

ISBN: 1-59182-314-5

First TOKYOPOP printing: May 2003

10 9 8 7 6 5 4

Printed in the USA

TABLE OF CONTENTS

AS MILITARY DICTATORSHIPS GO, IT COULD BE WORSE. BUT NOT BY MUCH. SHOW YOUR FACE AT A POLITICAL RALLY OR TWO, MOUTH THE STATE SPONSORED RHETORIC... WE GET BY.

WORK IS, AFTER ALL, WORK, WHATEVER GOVERNMENT YOU SERVE. AND SCHOOL IS SCHOOL. NOT THAT THAT'S A GOOD THING. SEE? WE GOT GOOD, WE GOT BAD. CAN YOU SAY ANY DIFFERENT?

危険思想的楽曲
厳禁

政府広報局

THOUGHT NOT. SPEAKING OF BAD, JUST HOPE YOU'RE NEVER SUBJECTED TO WHAT PASSES FOR MUSIC AROUND THESE PARTS. MUZAK, MORE LIKE. YOU WANNA ROCK, YOU BETTER GROW EYES IN THE BACK OF YOUR HEAD, KNOW WHAT I MEAN?

WHAT KIND OF GAME ARE WE TALKING HERE? PRIME-TIME BULLSHIT. I KID YOU NOT.

Chapter 1: The Worst Game in History

BATTLE ROYALE

BATTLE ROYALE

JIKEIKAN ORPHAN CARE FACILITY.
SHUUYA!

HURRY UP! IT'S COMING ON!

ALL RIGHT!

COME ON! IT'S STARTING!
MAXIMUM CARNAGE
TOO COOL, EH, YOSHITOKI? ♡
WAY COOL! ♡

WE INTERRUPT THIS PROGRAM FOR A SPECIAL REPORT. ATTEND.
DHK
HEY! NO FAIR!
THE PROGRAM SEASON FINALE WILL AIR TONIGHT AT 8:00 P.M. STANDARD TIME. ALL NON-ESSENTIAL SERVICES WILL BE SUSPENDED TO MAXIMIZE VIEWER PARTICIPATION IN THE EVENT.

......
AWWW... I WANNA SEE MAXIMUM CARNAGE.
A REMINDER THAT THE CONTESTANTS FOR THIS SEASON OF *THE PROGRAM* WERE CULLED FROM CLASS E CANDIDATES PUT FORWARD BY THE ADMINISTRATIVE STAFF OF THIRD WARD JUNIOR HIGH SCHOOL, KAGAWA DISTRICT. HONOR THEM IN THOUGHT AND DEED.
THIS SEASON'S WINNING CONTESTANT CAME CLOSE TO BREAKING THE '07 RECORD OF THREE DAYS, SEVEN HOURS AND TWENTY-TWO MINUTES SET BY FOURTEENTH WARD JUNIOR HIGH, MYOKI DISTRICT...
WE'RE MISSING OUR SHOW!
?
... MISSING THE RECORD BY A SCANT NINETEEN MINUTES. AH... I'M BEING TOLD WE HAVE LIVE COVERAGE OF...
YES. WE HAVE LIVE COVERAGE OF THE WINNING CONTESTANT BEING ESCORTED BY AN HONOR GUARD OF--
A GIRL! IT'S A YOUNG GIRL. THIS IS ONE FOR THE RECORD BOOKS!
HUH?

SHE LOOKS LIKE A MONSTER. SHUUYA, WHY DOES SHE LOOK LIKE A--
SHE'S NOT A MONSTER! SHE'S... SHE'S JUST LAUGHING.
fsk-t!
!
!
MS. RYOKO! OUR SHOW!
......
POOR CHILD...

UM... MS. RYOKO?
HRM?
!

ARE YOU TRYING TO BUY TIME, YOSHITOKI?

NO. I... WHEN WE GET TO NINTH GRADE, DO WE HAVE TO GO ON *THE PROGRAM* TOO?
THAT GIRL WAS LAUGHING, BUT I DON'T THINK SHE WAS HAPPY.

NO. SHE WASN'T.
I DON'T THINK YOU HAVE TO WORRY ABOUT *THE PROGRAM.* IT'S... LIKE A LOTTERY. A BAD LOTTERY.
ONE I WON'T LET YOU WIN.
PROMISE.

whir
......
BESIDES, DO YOU KNOW ANYONE WHO'S EVER WON A LOTTERY? EVEN A BAD ONE?
OF COURSE NOT. THE ODDS ARE WAY TOO HIGH.
EVEN HIGHER WITH ME HERE TO PROTECT YOU.

NO, MS. RYOKO.
YOSHITOKI AND I WILL PROTECT YOU. THAT'S WHAT MEN DO, PROTECT LADIES...
... AND YOSHITOKI AND I ARE MEN! WE'LL USE MAXIMUM CARNAGE!
!
!

......
YEAH! MAXIMUM CARNAGE! ULTIMATE POWER!

......
ULTIMATE POWER. YEAH...

......
THAT'S... COMFORTING TO KNOW, LITTLE WARRIORS.
......

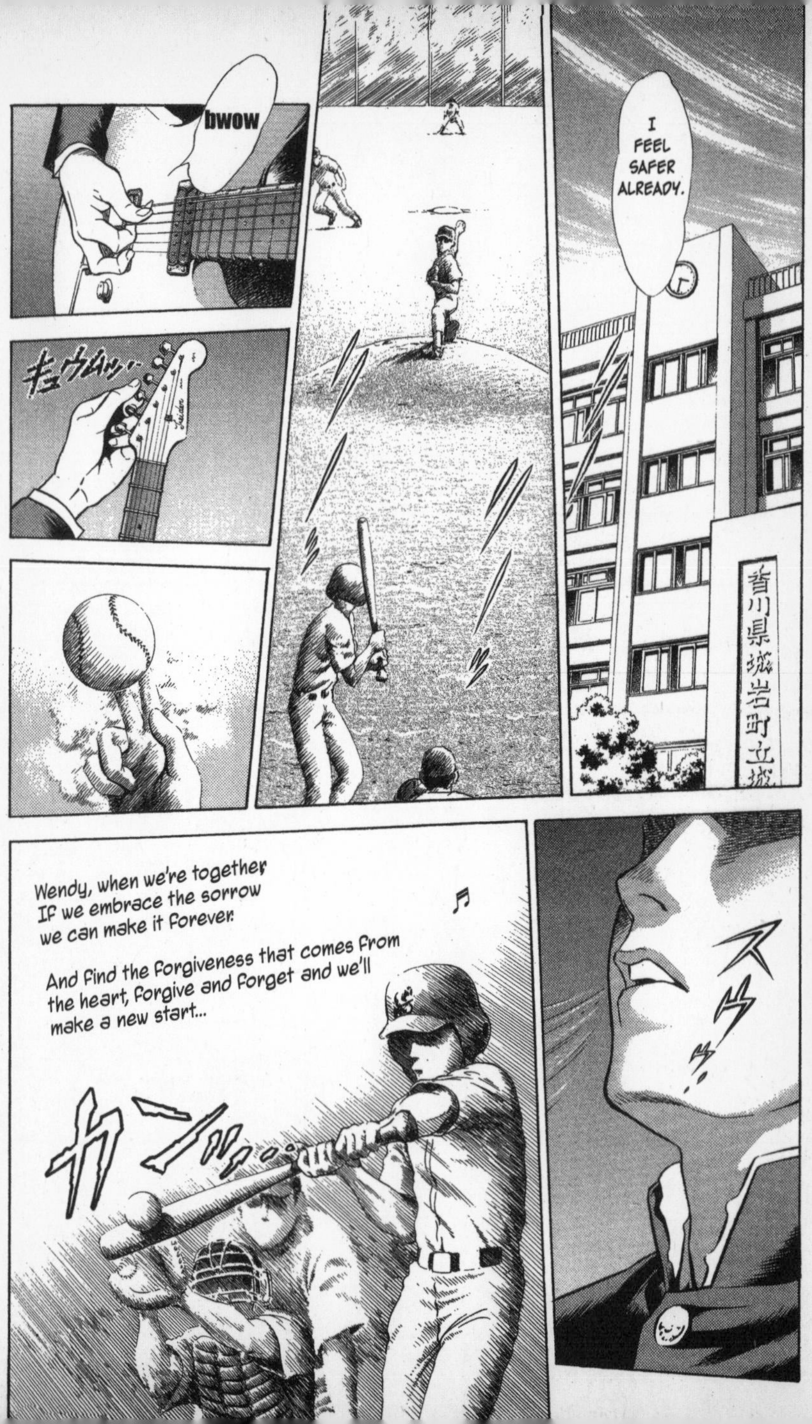

I FEEL SAFER ALREADY.

香川県城岩町立城

bwow

Wendy, when we're together,
If we embrace the sorrow
we can make it forever.

And find the forgiveness that comes from
the heart, forgive and forget and we'll
make a new start...

There will come a day you'll know that it's true... ♪
Know there's no one who loves you the way that I do... ♬
But until that day comes when you're back in my arms... ♬
Until we're no longer apart. Deprived of your charms, there's not much I can do... ♬
But live in the shadow cast over my heart. ♬
!!
SHUUYA!

YOU WANT TO HOLD IT DOWN TO A DULL ROAR?
OR DO YOU WANT THE WRONG EARS HEARING YOUR TONE-DEAF SCREECHING?

LEVEL WITH ME, YOSHI, WAS I NOT BORN TO ROCK? THAT'S ROCK AS IN ROLL, M'FRIEND, JUST IN CASE YOU HAVEN'T BEEN PAYING ATTENTION.

Ask me if I care, I'll tell you that I don't... ♪
Tell me that I gotta stop, you know damn well I won't... ♬

ROCK ON, YOSHI-TOKI.

......

LOOK AT YOU. ALL PARANOID AND WORRIED AND STILL LOVING EVERY NOTE OF IT.

TELL ME I'M WRONG.

NINTH GRADE/CLASS B - BOY #15:
SHUUYA NANAHARA

COULD I EVER?

NINTH GRADE/ CLASS B - BOY #7:
YOSHITOKI KUNINOBU

ダッ

ス
パシュッ
MI-MU-RA! RAH!
MI-MU-RA! RAH!
♡
キャーッ
キャーッ
キャーッ
キャーッ
HMMM...
HOW MANY CONDOMS SURVIVED THE PEP RALLY...?

1
2
3
4
×
×
TWO... FIVE... NO, FOUR...
SAY WHAT?
.....
キャーッ キャーッ
DAMN... NOT NEARLY ENOUGH.
BAD TIME TO COME UP WALLET LIGHT ON L'IL SHINJI'S RAINCOATS.
AND I DO SO HATE TO DISAPPOINT A CUTE GIRL... WHAT THE HELL, I'LL IMPROVISE.

NINTH GRADE/CLASS B - BOY #19:

SHINJI MIMURA

ズッ…

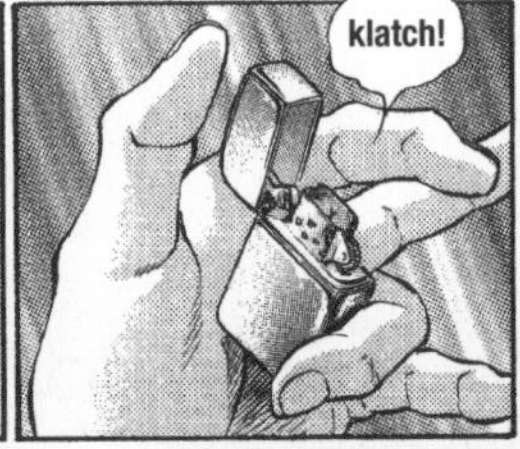
klatch!

SIGH…

ISN'T THAT THE TRANSFER KID? FROM CLASS B?
YEAH. STEER CLEAR. THAT'S ONE TOUGH CUSTOMER.
STRONG SILENT TYPE, Y'KNOW? ATTITUDE TO SPARE.
HE SEEMS A BIT... I DUNNO... BIG FOR JUNIOR HIGH?

DIDN'T YOU HEAR? HE'S A JUVEE BOUNCE.
GOT IN OVER HIS HEAD AT HIS LAST SCHOOL.

MESSED WITH THE WRONG CROWD. GOT HIMSELF DAMN NEAR KILLED.
WOUND UP MISSING MOST OF THE YEAR AND GOT LEFT BACK. "LUCKY" US HE WOUND UP HERE, EH?
.....
NINTH GRADE/CLASS B - BOY #5:
SHOGO KAWADA

NINTH GRADE/CLASS B - BOY #11:
HIROKI SUGIMURA

HA!!
CLUB
WHUFF!

HNGH... HNGH... MY ARM... SON OF... HNGH... OF A BITCH BROKE MY ARM...
WAY TO GO, BOSS.
DEAD BANG!
NOT ...
NOT SMART, KID... YAKUZA DON'T TAKE TO... TO PUNK-ASS KIDS...
BOUGHT YOURSELF A WORLD OF TROUBLE, PUNK ASS.

BOSS?! YOU?! BUT YOU... YOU'RE JUST A... A KID!
......
BAR BARON
カラオケ 南海亭
ビデオ・本
NINTH GRADE/CLASS B - BOY #6:
KAZUO KIRIYAMA
A KID?
DO I LOOK LIKE A KID TO YOU?
THERE... YOU SEE? IT'S ALL A MATTER OF PERSPECTIVE, ISN'T IT?
♡
YOU LIKE?

MMM?
HOW MUCH DO YOU LIKE, LITTLE MAN?
NINTH GRADE/CLASS B - GIRL #11:
MITSUKO SOUMA
TELL ME!
A PEEK... JUST A PEEK OF PINK...
NAME IT! NAME YOUR PRICE! I... I...
TELL ME AND IT'S YOURS.
ANYTHING! PLEASE!
SO.
WE UNDERSTAND ONE ANOTHER, EH, LITTLE MAN? ♡

NINTH GRADE/CLASS B - GIRL #15:

NORIKO NAKAGAWA

SHE "KINDA" GOT A NAME?

♪

そろっ
♬

パク
HUH?

NOT AGAIN!
HEH HEH HEH... THAT MAKES FOUR!

DO I HAVE TO POST A GUARD?
THESE COOKIES ARE FOR SCHOOL TOMORROW. I'LL MAKE YOU A BATCH IF YOU PROMISE TO LEAVE THESE ALONE.

キュウ
YOU COULDN'T HAVE TIMED IT BETTER, YOSHI.
WHAT WITH TOMORROW BEING THE GRADUATION TRIP AND ALL.

HUH?
WHAT'S THAT SUPPOSED TO MEAN?

Oh, baby though I can't tell you how I feel cause I'm pretty much a dork with a limited vocabulary...
!!
... and social skills that are the shame of my family. So my friend here wrote a song to tell you how I feel...
...just don't get the hots for him cause he's so much better looking than me...
OH YEAH.
NOT FUNNY, SHU! BESIDES... IT'S NOT LIKE I'M READY TO... I MEAN, SHE'S NOT ...

RIBBED...
RIBBED?!
NYUK NYUK NYUK...
BOYS?

BOYS! IT'S GETTING A BIT LATE FOR THAT KIND OF RACKET.
I'D JUST AS SOON REMAIN ON GOOD TERMS WITH THE NEIGHBORS...
IF IT'S ALL THE SAME TO YOU.

MS. RYOKO, HAVE YOU HEARD?
LOVE IS IN THE AIR.
♡ ♡
OUR LITTLE YOSHITOKI'S COME DOWN WITH A BAD CASE OF THE SCREAMING THIGH SWEATS.
SHUUYA! NO! DON'T LISTEN TO HIM! HE'S DELUSIONAL!

SHUUYA, WOULD YOU JUST SHUT THE HELL UP!

YOU NEED ANYTHING, JUST SAY THE WORD, BOSS.

C'MON, YOSHI. IS THAT ANY WAY TO BE?
I SAID I WAS SORRY. LOOK. LOOK HOW SINCERE I AM.
SHUUYA?

UM... YESTERDAY MY PAIN-IN-THE-A... BUTT LITTLE BROTHER BEGGED ME TO BAKE UP A BATCH OF COOKIES FOR HIM AND...
THERE WERE, AH... SOME LEFT OVER AND YOU KNOW HOW COOKIES GET IF THEY... IF THEY SIT TOO LONG?
I THOUGHT YOU MIGHT... I MEAN, YOU AND YOSHITOKI MIGHT LIKE--

REALLY? WOW! YOU MADE THEM YOURSELF?
THAT IS SO COOL! NO, REALLY, THEY MUST BE REALLY GOOD.

MM-MMM... YUP. I KNEW IT. REALLY GOOD. REALLY. ♡
THAT'S SO SWEET OF YOU TO SAY. ♡

YO, DON JUAN, DIAL IT DOWN A FEW.
"KINDA" DOES HAVE A NAME...

......
PSST... SHOULD I GET MY GUITAR?

RIBBED?!
HOO

ZZZZ...
?
HEY, YOSHI ?
!!

HUH...
ZZZ-MNF...
WHAT'S... NORIKO TOO?
WHAT'D YOU PUT IN THEM COOKIES, GIRL?
WHAT...
COOKIES...
WHUZZA... HAPPEN...
HNGH... LOOKA THA'...

EVER'BODY SLEEPIN'... HOW'S THAT? WHAT KINDA CLASS TRIP... EVER'BODY FALLS ASLEEP?
HEY, EVER'BODY... CALL THIS A GRADU... LATION TRIP? HELLO?
'KAY... OKAY. MEBBE... MEBBE I TAKE A NAP TOO... SOUN' RIGHT...
ZZZZ...

HMM...? KAWADA?
WHA'S HE...?

!!
N-NGH...
DAMN... THEM TO...
...HELL ...GN NNN ...
WHA'S ...
TRY'N BREAK WIN'OW?
GET HI'SEF BIG TROUBLE ...
CAN' JUS' BREAK WIN'OW ONNA BUS...
HEY...
LOOKA BUS 'RIVER... GOT SE'F A... LIKE A GAS MASK?

WHA'S UP WI' THAT?

LOOK LIKE A SPACE... SPACE ALIEN'R SUM'IN...

'R LIKE ONNA AIRPLANE... LIKE A OSHEGEN MAS'...

LADIES AN' GEM'IN... IN CASE OF CABIN DECOM... DECOMPRESHEN' WE GOT THESE HERE OSHEGEN MAS' GONNA HE'P YOU ALL BREEVE...

JUS' STRAP ONNA MAS' WHEN IT DROPS AND YOU BE HUNKY DORY A-OKAYYYY... 'SPECIALLY YOU BE DRIVIN' TH' BUS... HOWZAT FAIR? BUS DRIVER GETS A OSHEGEN MAS' AN' WE DON'...

DON' SEEM FAIR T' ME... NOT... FAIR...

... AT ALL...

......

SHUUYA? AND YOSHITOKI? THE WHOLE CLASS?!
I CAN'T...
I... I WON'T ACCEPT THIS!

HOW DARE YOU!
THOSE POOR BOYS!
RYOKO!
NO! I WON'T HAVE IT! DO YOU HEAR ME!?
THEY'VE DONE NOTHING TO DESERVE THIS! NOTHING!

I WILL NOT HAVE THOSE BOYS PUNISHED FOR BEING ORPHANS!
......
SIGH...
TYPICAL.

!!
!!
ALL OF US?
HEY! MY WATCH! SOMEBODY STOLE MY...
WHERE IS... WHERE ARE WE?
IS THIS A CLASSROOM? ARE WE BACK AT SCHOOL?
HOW COULD ALL OF US FALL ASLEEP AT THE SAME...
DOES ANYONE KNOW HOW LONG WE WERE OUT? WHAT TIME IS IT NOW?
SOMEONE'S SCREWING WITH OUR HEADS. THAT'S GOTTA BE...
AH, GEEZ, THERE GOES YUKIO, TURNING ON THE WATERWORKS. GET A GRIP, GIRL.
SINCE WHEN ARE OUR FLOORS WOOD? CHECK IT OUT!
......
WHAT IS THIS? IT'S LIKE A DOJO WITH DESKS.

YO!
YOSHITOKI. OVER HERE.
?
NORIKO. HEY, NORIKO...
HUH?
WHAT'S ...
IS THAT A COLLAR?
HUH.
......
UH-HUH...
UH-HUH.
!!
SUNNUVA! TAGGED ME TOO!?
NOT GOOD. MOST DEFINITELY NOT GOOD.
LADIES. GENTLEMEN. IF YOU'LL PLEASE SETTLE DOWN.
IF I CAN HAVE YOUR ATTENTION, PLEASE...
!!

NO LINGERING ILL EFFECTS, I HOPE?
SHOULDN'T BE. THE GAS WAS DESIGNED TO BE FREE OF LINGERING AFTER-EFFECTS.
skreet
kreech
嘉門
CAN'T HAVE YOU HUNG OVER, CAN WE?
WH ...?
WHO THE HELL IS THAT?
I SHOULD KNOW?
嘉門米美
SO. WE BEGIN. I AM YOUR NEW TEACHER. MY NAME IS YONEMI KAMON.
YOU MAY CALL ME "SIR."
THAT SAID, LET ME BE THE FIRST TO WELCOME YOU TO OUR LITTLE COMPETITION. ♡
ATTEN-TIVE. VERY GOOD.
AN ATTENTIVE CLASS IS AN EFFICIENT CLASS. AS FIRST IMPRESSIONS GO, VERY GOOD!
KEEP THIS UP AND WE CAN SPARE OURSELVES ANY... UNPLEASANTNESS DOWN THE LINE.

IS THIS GUY SERIOUS ?
COMPETITION? LIKE A GAME?
GET REAL!
?
SO ...
I THINK YOU'LL FIND THE NEXT FEW DAYS... INTERESTING, TO SAY THE LEAST.
SOME AMONG YOU MIGHT EVEN "GET OFF ON IT," TO USE THE VERNACULAR.
IT'S ALL A MATTER OF PERSONAL PREFERENCE.
stomp
SOME OPT FOR FOOLHARDY COURAGE, OTHERS, DELIBERATE CAUTION.
STILL OTHERS, CRAVEN COWARDICE.
THERE ARE STOIC LONERS AND THOSE WHO FIND STRENGTH IN NUMBERS.
skritch
I WOULD ADVISE AGAINST THAT EXCEPT AS A TEMPORARY NECESSITY.
YES...
?
FRIENDS, I'M SORRY TO SAY, ALL TOO SOON BECOME LIABILITIES. TRUST, FRAGILE.
THIS... IT CAN'T BE...
SANITY EVEN MORE FRAGILE.
AH, AH... I NEVER SAID IT WOULD BE EASY.

FORTY-TWO COMPETE UNTIL A WINNER IS DETERMINED.

SURVIVAL OF THE FITTEST... OR SO WE LIKE TO BELIEVE.

KILL OR BE KILLED.
DO UNTO OTHERS ...

... JUST BE SURE YOU MAKE IT STICK. ♡
......
THE PROGRAM!
WE'RE GOING TO BE ON THE PROGRAM!
YOSHITOKI... NORIKO... I-I CAN'T...
WOULD THEY? COULD THEY? GOD HELP US... THE FUCKING PROGRAM!
BASTARDS!

: Noriko Nakagawa 8: Kayoko Kotohiki 1: Mizuho Inada 15: Shuuya Nanahara 8: Yoji Kuramoto 1: Yoshio Akamatsu

: Yuka Nakagawa 9: Yuko Sakaki 2: Yukio Utsumi 16: Kazushi Niida 9: Hiroshi Kuronaga 2: Keita Iijima

7: Satomi Noda 10: Hirono Shimizu 3: Megumi Etou 17: Mitsuru Numai 10: Ryuhei Sasagawa 3: Tatsumichi Ooki

: Fumiyo Fujiyoshi 11: Mitsuko Souma 4: Sakura Ogawai 18: Tadakatsu Hatagami 11: Hiroki Sugimura 4: Toshinori Oda

9: Chisato Matsui 12: Haruka Tanizawa 5: Izumi Kanai 19: Shinji Mimura 12: Yutaka Sato 5: Shogo Kawada

20: Kaori Minami 13: Takako Chigusa 6: Yukiko Kitano 20: Kyoichi Motobuchi 13: Yuichiro Takiguchi 6: Kazuo Kiriyama

: Yoshimi Yahagi 14: Mayumi Tendo 7: Yumiko Kusaka 21: Kazuhiko Yamamoto 14: Sho Tsukioka 7: Yoshitoki Kuninobu

DO UNTO OTHERS ...

Chapter 2: Best Friend
FORTY-TWO COMPETE UNTIL ONLY ONE REMAINS.
BASIC SUBTRACTION, CLASS. FORTY-TWO MINUS FORTY-ONE...
NO TAKERS? HRMM... JUST AS WELL. ♡

明日を支える
専守防衛軍
入隊希望者
随時募集中!!
明日を支える
専守防衛軍
入隊希望者
随時募集中!!
明日を支える
専守防衛軍
入隊希望者
随時募集中!!
... PROGRAM... CHOSEN FOR THE PROGRAM... CAN'T... **WON'T...** HOW COULD THIS HAPPEN...?

NO!
!!

NO! NOT ME! THERE'S BEEN A MISTAKE!
!!

TYPICAL.

?!
KYOICHI! SIT DOWN, FOOL!

MY FATHER... HE WORKS FOR THE GOVERNMENT. DIRECTOR OF... OF ENVIRONMENTAL AFFAIRS.
HN...
HN...
YOU SEE? YOU'VE GOT THE WRONG CLASS. MY... MY FATHER WOULD NEVER ALLOW...
HN...

SO, CLASS PRESIDENT MOTOBUCHI, WHAT HAVE WE LEARNED SO FAR?

WE HAVE *LEARNED...* HAVE WE NOT, CLASS PRESIDENT MOTOBUCHI?
I...
I ...
I AM ...
I AM AMONG... EQUALS. SIR.
EXCEL-LENT. MOST EXCEL-LENT. ♡
ESPECIALLY LIKED THE "SIR." VERY GOOD.

ON-WARD THEN.
IN CASE ANY OF YOU WERE WONDERING, YOUR PARENTS, GUARDIANS, WHATEVER, HAVE BEEN NOTIFIED ABOUT YOUR PARTICI-PATION...
THEY SEND THEIR BEST WISHES... LOVE, KISSES, YADDA, BAH... THAT WOULD BE EXCEPTING THOSE GLAD TO BE RID OF YOU. YOU KNOW WHO YOU ARE.
DO THEM PROUD, LITTLE WARRIORS, IF ONLY TO RUB THEIR FACES IN YOUR VICTORY. ♡

OH...
OH
DEAR.

A BIT MUCH TO TAKE IN IN ONE SITTING, I KNOW.
STILL... CAN'T HAVE YOU ZONING OUT ON ME.

I KNOW.
PERHAPS A VISUAL AID WILL HELP MOVE THINGS ALONG.

klatch

!?
A BODY BAG... MOST DEFINITELY NOT GOOD...

.....
?
?
?

SO ...
THE SUSPENSE IS KILLING YOU? ATTEND. ♡
zzzzip

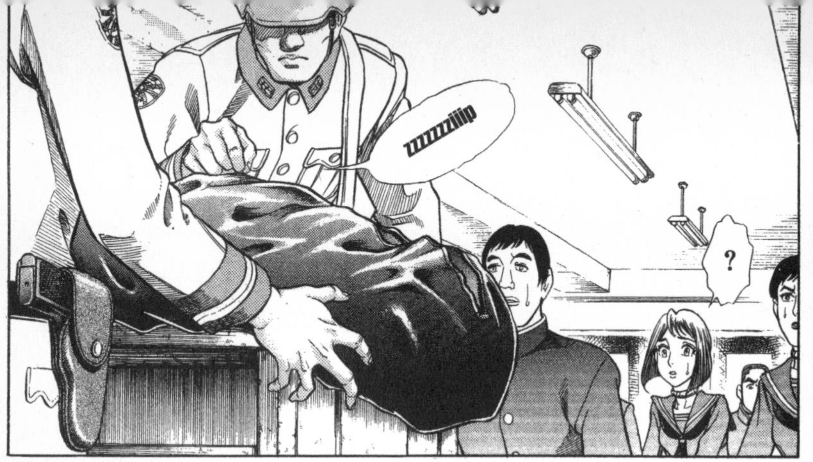
zzzzzzziiip
?

HEH...
HEH...
HEH ...
HEH- H...

MR. HAYASHIDAAAAA !!!
キャアッ…!
MR. HAYASHIDA ...
HLG-GG...
WH-WHAT?!
GLARK ...

AREN'T YOU SOMETHING? RECOGNIZED HIM AS YOUR TEACHER...

EVEN WITH THE MODIFI-CATIONS MADE TO HIS APPEARANCE.

♡

SUCH A SPECIAL GIRL. YOU'D BE OUR LITTLE MISS NAKAGAWA, NO?

♡

AND DOES OUR LITTLE MISS NAKAGAWA KNOW WHY MR. HAYASHIDA JOINED US TODAY?

♡

MR. HAYASHIDA WAS DEAD SET AGAINST THIS CLASS PARTICIPATING IN THE PROGRAM. NOT QUITE AS VOCAL AS HIS ORPHANAGE WHORE, BUT THEN FEW TONGUES CUT SHARPER THAN A WOMAN'S.

OH ...

NO OFFENSE.

H-HEH ...

H-HEH ...

THINK, GODDAMN YOU, THINK!!

!!
UM... SIR?
!!
SIR ... I...
SHUT UP!
YOSHI ...
SIT DOWN AND SHUT UP, YOSHITOKI.
SHUT UP AND SIT DOWN! PLEASE!
SPIT IT OUT, YOUNG MASTER.
YOU HAD ME AT "SIR." ♡

I...

I HAVE NO PARENTS.

WHO DID YOU TELL... ABOUT THIS? ABOUT ME?

AH... ONE OF THE ORPHAN BOYS.

A CAULDRON OF SUBVERSIVE THINK, OUR WELFARE SYSTEM. AND AFTER ALL WE GIVE...

!!

PROOF POSITIVE THAT NO GOOD DEED GOES UNPUNISHED.

SO DELECTABLE...
SUCH A DELICATE BEAUTY ... ♡
ペロ
!
YOU SEE? I SMILE TO REMEMBER HER.
SIGH... IT'S ALWAYS THE SUBVERSIVE ONES.
!
WH...
WHA...
WHAT DID YOU DO TO MS. RYOKO?
MMM ... ♡
TOUGH LOVE, YOUNG MASTER.
BUT THEN, IS THERE ANY OTHER KIND?

SO PINK, YOUNG MASTER...
... AND GIVEN PROPER... PERSUASION ...

... MORE THAN WILLING TO SHARE IT. ♡

ドクーン
ドクーン
SORRY. SORRY. GOT LOST IN THE MEMORY.
NOW THEN, WHERE WERE WE?

MS...
MS. RYOKO...
NO, MS. RYOKO.
YOSHITOKI AND I WILL PROTECT YOU. THAT'S WHAT MEN DO, PROTECT LADIES...
... AND YOSHITOKI AND I ARE MEN!
MS. RYOKO...
.....
YEAH! MAXIMUM CARNAGE! ULTIMATE POWER! ♡
ULTIMATE POWER. YEAH!

......
THAT'S... COMFORTING TO KNOW, LITTLE WARRIORS.
MORE THAN WILLING TO SHARE IT.
I FEEL SAFER ALREADY.
MORE THAN WILLING ...
... SO PINK...
... MORE THAN WILLING ...
... SHARE IT...

YOU... COLD BLOODED BASTARD!
I'LL RIP OFF YOUR HEAD...
AND SHIT DOWN YOUR THROAT, YOU MISERABLE SON OF A BITCH!

STEADY, LITTLE WARRIOR.

......

THREATEN ME, YOU THREATEN THE GOVERNMENT. YOU MIGHT WANT TO RETHINK THIS.

HONESTLY
...

DID YOU REALLY THINK THE BITCH WAS SAVING IT FOR THE LIKES OF YOU?

SHUT UP!

I'LL KILL YOU! I'LL KILL YOU! I'LL KILL YOU! I'LL...

HE'S YOUR BEST FRIEND! DO SOMETHING! STOP THINKING ABOUT IT AND--

YOSHITOKI! NO! DON'T DO IT!

My best friend... always there... always caring...
That's the way, Shuuya!
Hey, Shuuya!
That is so you, Shuuya.
Always there when no one else was... always that dopey Yoshi smile...
Never a bad word...
Only ever seen him angry twice...
The orphanage dog. Eddie. Stupid name for a dog. Car hit him... Yoshi chased that car six blocks before his legs gave out...
You killed Eddie! Stop him! Somebody stop...
Yoshi!
Gasp... Yoshi!
You shut up! You shut up and go! Now!
Second time was that collections agent. Came around smart-mouthing Ms. Ryoko...
Third time's the charm... my ass!

SIGH... I CAN SEE YOU'RE DETERMINED TO SEE THIS THROUGH. ATTEND CLASS, THE FIRST ONE'S ON ME. ♡

I, UM... I THINK I FOUND A GIRL I KINDA LIKE.
!
KINDA? SHE "KINDA" GOT A NAME?
!
YO ...
YOSHI... I DIDN'T PUT IT TOGETHER ...
I THOUGHT IT WAS NORIKO.

YOSHITOKI!
NOOOOOOOOOOOOO!

SINCE WE WERE KIDS...
YOSHITOKI... HE'S ALWAYS THERE. IN EVERY MEMORY WORTH REVISITING... HE'S ALWAYS THERE.

ALWAYS SMILING THAT BIG, DOPEY YOSHI SMILE...
... AND LAUGHING THAT CONTAGIOUS YOSHI LAUGH.

MY BEST FRIEND ...

THERE FOR ME WHENEVER IT COUNTED ...
... WHENEVER I NEEDED HIM...

Chapter 3: Shinji Mimura

AND WHEN HE MOST ***NEEDED*** ME? WHERE WAS I WHEN HE ***MOST*** NEEDED ME?!
NO...
TOO FAST... IT ALL HAPPENED TOO FAST. I COULDN'T... COULDN'T...
A-HUH...
I COULDN'T MOVE. I COULDN'T BE THERE FOR HIM!
MY BEST FRIEND...
YOSHI...

NO SWEAT, SHUUYA.
SHU ...
SHU ...
THAT IS SO YOU, SHUUYA!!
SHU ...
CAN'T ...
I CAN'T ...

YOSHITOKI!!

!

YOSHI? YOSHI-TOKI?
!

SIGH... SOME NEVER LEARN.

!!

NORIKO TOO?!
NO...

NORIKO!!

EEEEEEEEEE

STAY DOWN! STAY DOWN, NORIKO!

LISTEN TO YOUR FRIEND OR THE NEXT SHOT COUNTS. ♡

FYI, AND WERE YOU NOT THE LEAST BIT DISCIPLINED I WOULDN'T HAVE TO EMPHASIZE THIS...

NO ONE LEAVES THEIR SEAT WITHOUT TEACHER'S PERMISSION.

PLEASE, SIR?

HMM?

PLEASE HELP HIM...
YOSHITOKI... *PLEASE* HELP HIM, SIR.
SHU...
SHU...
SHU...
......
ポカンッ..
NOT NORIKO TOO...
......

...UK ... HOO ...

ÜK ...

HARD LESSONS ARE BEST LEARNED AT ANOTHER'S EXPENSE.

THAT'S, PRETTY MUCH WHAT I HAD IN MIND.

I SHOULD FINISH WHAT I STARTED. ♡

GASP!
DO YOU SEE?
THERE IS DARK BEAUTY HERE, IF YOU'VE AN EYE FOR IT. ♡

YOU PSYCHOTIC SON OF A BITCH!
NO MORE!
NO FUCKING MORE!

AHHHHHHHHHHHH
!
KILLYOUYOU SICKPSYCHO BASTARD!!
SHUUYA! NO!
WHAT DO YOU KNOW... ELVIS LIVES.
BUT NOT FOR LONG IF HE DOESN'T PLANT HIS ASS BACK AT HIS DESK.

YOU'LL THANK ME FOR THIS LATER.
IF WE LIVE.
!

THUDDA-WHUMP
.....
MI...

MIMURA!

SIGH... LET ME GET THIS STRAIGHT ...

THE MAN WITH THE GUN SAYS STAY IN YOUR SEAT AND YOU TAKE THAT TO MEAN...

... JUMP AROUND THE ROOM LIKE DEMENTED GRASSHOPPERS?
MIMURA!
HE... HE STANDS BY ME!
THE WAY I SHOULD HAVE WITH YOSHI.
....
DOES HE DIE TOO? DO THE BOTH OF US DIE NOW?

THE TWO OF YOU WILL RETURN TO YOUR SEATS. NOW!

Chapter 4: The Oath

カッ カッ
カッ
カッ
スゥ…

HOW MUCH PER DEAD BODY?

HOW MUCH DO THEY DEDUCT FROM YOUR FEE FOR EVERY... "CONTESTANT" YOU TAKE DOWN?

YOU SAID FORTY-TWO START THE GAME. YOU'RE ALREADY DOWN TO FORTY-ONE.
HOW MUCH DO YOU FORFEIT AT FORTY? THIRTY-NINE? I'M GUESSING THE ***PENALTIES*** RUN KIND OF STEEP.
AND HOW BADLY ARE THE RATINGS AFFECTED IF THERE ARE TOO FEW OF US TO MAKE A RUN AT THE '07 RECORD?
BET THERE'S ALL KINDS OF PENALTIES FOR ***FUCKING*** UP THAT PARTICULAR CASH COW.

THEY PAY YOU TO SEE TO IT WE DIE OUT THERE. IN FRONT OF THE CAMERAS.
I'M THINKING YOU MIGHT WANT TO RECONSIDER YOUR MOTIVATIONAL TACTICS...

"SIR"...

BWAH HAAAA!
HA HA HAAA !
PRICELESS! HAHA HAAA...
HAHA HAAA... HAHA HAAA... HAHA HAAA...
HE'S PLAYING US... THE SADISTIC BASTARD!
PLAYING US!
AHEH.
AND SO WELL THOUGHT OUT. I ALMOST BOUGHT INTO IT MYSELF! ♡

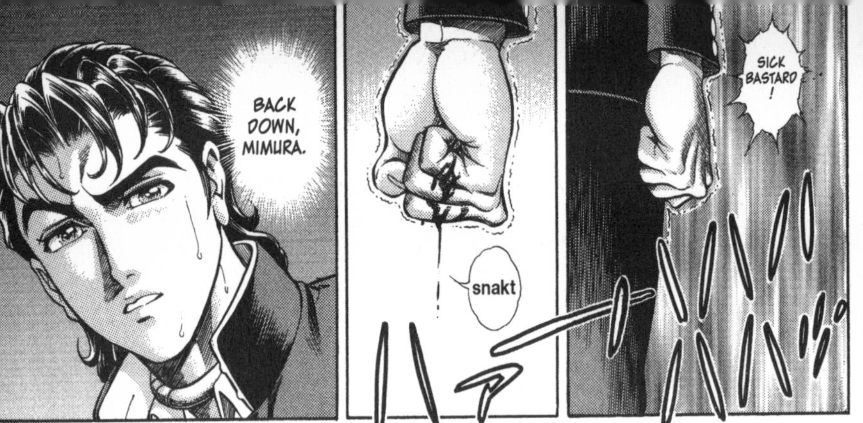
SICK BASTARD!
snakt
BACK DOWN, MIMURA.
MOST EXCELLENT, YOUNG MASTER... WHOEVER. IT'S BEEN A WHILE SINCE I'VE ENJOYED A GOOD LAUGH.
NOW SIT DOWN BEFORE I FORGET I'M IN A GOOD MOOD. ♡
SIR!
THERE IS SOMETHING ELSE.
BE QUICK.
I'M BEGINNING TO REMEMBER WHY I LOATHE TEENAGERS.
IT'S JUST... THE ODDS ARE LOPSIDED. IN FAVOR OF A GIRL WINNING. ONE OF THE BOYS... YOU SHOT HIM AND...
WELL... FORTY-ONE DOESN'T BREAK DOWN... IT'S NOT AN EVEN MATCH. YOU SEE? NORIKO'S JUST WOUNDED.

MIMURA ... WHAT ...?
WHAT IS HE...?
I SEE... MALE PRIDE. YES...
PERHAPS WE SHOULD POSTPONE UNTIL A REPLACEMENT BOY CAN BE FOUND... EH? ♡
!!
AND WHILE WE'RE AT IT, CLEAR THE AIR OF ANY MISCONCEPTIONS ABOUT YOUR LIVES BEING OF ANY WORTH TO ME. ♡
BETTER STILL...
LET'S JUST EVEN UP THE ODDS HERE AND NOW.
!!

WAIT! ARE WE NOT MEN?
WHAT DOES ONE EXTRA GIRL MATTER?
DELIGHTFUL! ♡
AND SO FAUX MACHO! NOW GET THE FUCK BACK TO YOUR DESK. ♡

ガタッ!!

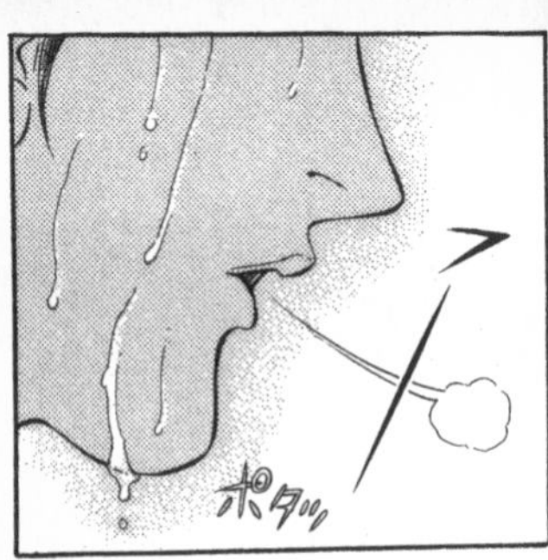
ポタッ

CLOSE
...
TOO
CLOSE.

ATTEND. MIMURA WAS, IN HIS OWN WAY, RIGHT ABOUT THE GAME BEING SOMEWHAT LOPSIDED.
BUT IT HAS NOTHING TO DO WITH GENDER. ABILITY. IT'S ALL ABOUT INHERENT ABILITY.
WHICH VARIES FROM PERSON TO PERSON, EH?

PSST
...
YUKI
...

UNBELIEVABLE!
NO TALKING DURING CLASS SHOULD BE A GIVEN!
!!
!!
NNN ...

NNNOOOO...

GHK...

THERE YOU GO. A PERFECT EXAMPLE OF INHERENT ABILITY...

... AS IN THE YOUNG LADY'S INHERENT ABILITY TO AGGRAVATE THE TEACHER. ♡

TO CONTINUE. YOUR ABILITIES ALREADY RENDER YOU UNEQUAL.

SAD BUT TRUE.

THIS LACK OF... PARITY IS A BIG PART OF THE PROGRAM'S APPEAL.

CATTLE...

THAT'S ALL WE ARE TO HIM.

CATTLE FOR HIS SLAUGHTER-HOUSE PROGRAM.

THE UNDERDOG TRIUMPHING OVER NEAR-IMPOSSIBLE CIRCUMSTANCES... YOU KNOW THE DRILL.
"FAIR" DOES NOT ENTER INTO THIS. YOU MIGHT WANT TO KEEP THAT IN MIND.

ぴらっ

?
swif ...
?
klat!

SO
...
BEFORE WE GET INTO THE RULES AND REGULATIONS
...
TAKE UP YOUR PENCILS AND WRITE...

"I WILL KILL," FOLLOWED BY THE NAME OF A CLASSMATE.
REPEAT UNTIL ALL OF YOUR CLASSMATES HAVE BEEN NAMED.
♡

HE'S GETTING OFF ON THIS... PERVERT FUCK!
UP HIS! I'M NOT WRITING SHIT!

....
THEN WHAT?
BUY A BULLET TO THE HEAD?

NO. FOLLOW MIMURA'S LEAD.
PLAY ALONG... CHOOSE THE MOMENT TO... TO... TO WHAT?

TO MAKE UP FOR YOSHI
...

NORIKO
...

......

HUH ...

......

SMILE FOR ME, YOSHI ...

I'VE NEVER NEEDED IT MORE.
HEY, SHUUYA!
HEY, SHUUYA! OVER HERE!
UH-OH... THAT'S NOT A HAPPY YOSHI FACE.
I BEEN THINKING...
ABOUT GI-IRRRLS, I BET.

I THINK ABOUT MORE THAN GIRLS!
YOU WANT TO KISS AND HUG AND MARRY THEM AND HAVE A MILLION BABIES AND--
NO. NO BABIES. EVER.
......
EVER?
I LIKE IT THE WAY THEY SHOW IT ON TV. THE FAMILIES.
ON TV THE PARENTS ALWAYS LOVE THEIR KIDS. Y'KNOW?
THE MOM AND THE DAD AND... AND THE GRAN'MA ...
THEY REALLY LOVE THE KIDS A LOT.
IT'S NOT RE-EAL ...
ON TV THEY KEEP THEIR KIDS. LOVE THEM.
I DON'T CARE!
!

......
JEEZ, YOSHI ...
THAT'S WHY I LIKE THE GIRLS ON TV BETTER.
IF THEY MAKE A BABY, THEY KEEP IT. NOT LIKE... Y'KNOW... GIRLS.
....
UM ... OKAY ...
I DIDN'T GET IT BACK THEN... TOO YOUNG...
TOO STUPID. IT WAS SO EASY TO BLAME IT ALL ON GIRLS. WHAT DID WE KNOW?
skrit... skrit...
AHHH... DAMN!!
WHY AM I DREDGING ALL OF THIS UP NOW!?

SHUUYA? I THINK I FOUND A GIRL...
... I KINDA LIKE.
NORIKO! IT WAS *SUPPOSED* TO BE NORIKO!

YOU WERE MY ***BEST*** FRIEND! I WAS SUPPOSED TO KNOW YOU!
KINDA?

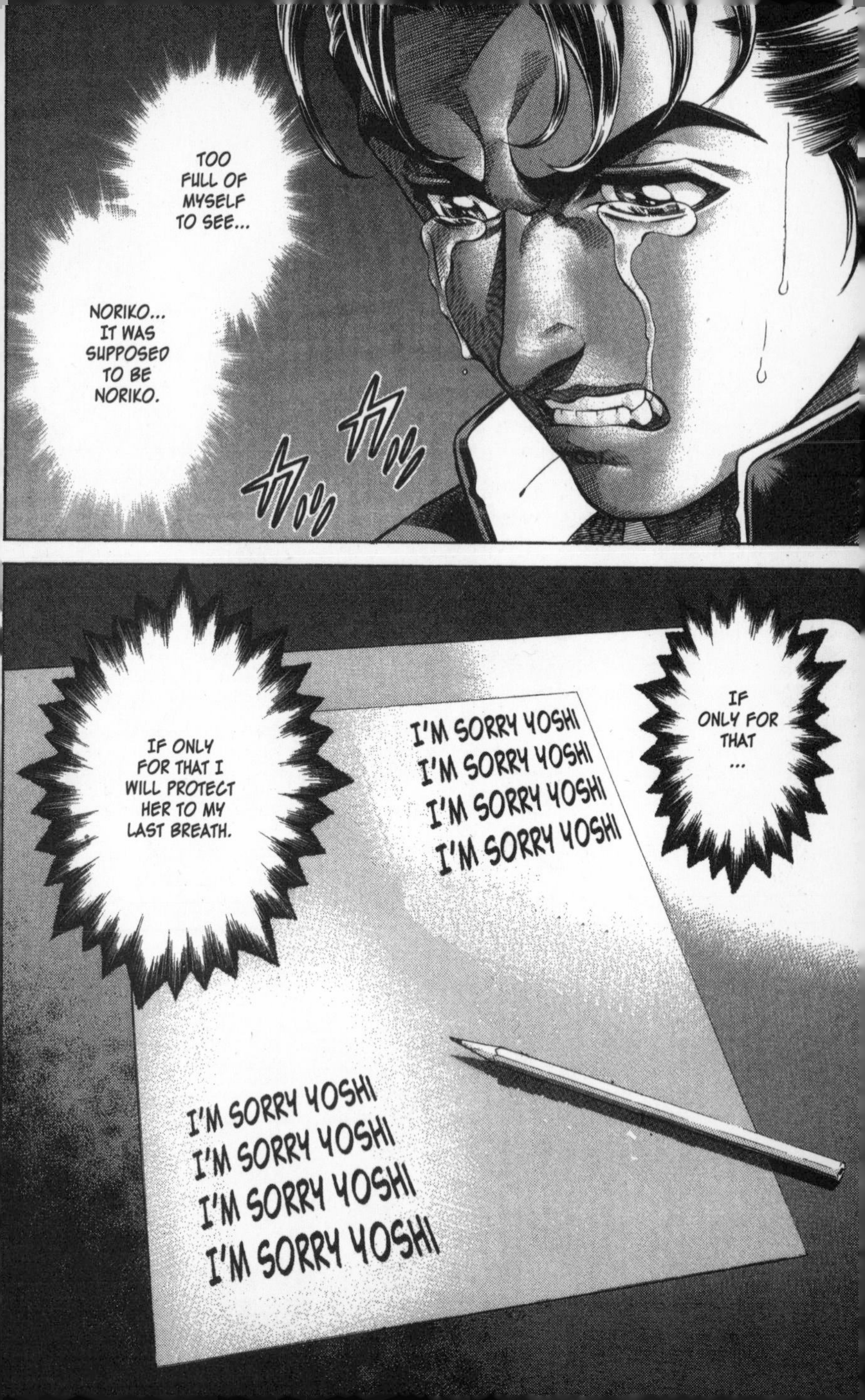

TOO FULL OF MYSELF TO SEE...
NORIKO... IT WAS SUPPOSED TO BE NORIKO.
IF ONLY FOR THAT ...
I'M SORRY YOSHI
I'M SORRY YOSHI
I'M SORRY YOSHI
I'M SORRY YOSHI
IF ONLY FOR THAT I WILL PROTECT HER TO MY LAST BREATH.
I'M SORRY YOSHI
I'M SORRY YOSHI
I'M SORRY YOSHI
I'M SORRY YOSHI

Chapter 5: Other Side Of The Door

SCREE - EE - SCREE - EE -
NOW WHAT ?
?

ATTEND.
THESE ARE YOUR SUPPLY PACKS. ONE FOR EACH OF YOU.
WITHIN YOU WILL FIND WATER, FIELD RATIONS, A MAP, COMPASS, WATCH...
... AND A RANDOMLY SELECTED WEAPON WITH WHICH YOU WILL...

EACH BAG CONTAINS A DIFFERENT WEAPON, VARIETY BEING THE SPICE OF LIFE. OR SO I'VE HEARD.
WHY BELABOR THE OBVIOUS, EH?
......

WEAPONS RANGE FROM KNIVES TO SEMIAUTOMATIC MACHINE GUNS, PLUS THE ODD SURPRISE OR TWO.
THE YOUNG LADIES MIGHT WANT TO LAY HANDS ON A FIRING WEAPON AS SOON AS POSSIBLE. ♡
......
THE YOUNG GENTLEMEN MIGHT WANT TO TAKE NOTE THAT THE LAST WINNER WAS A GIRL.
MALE PRIDE, GENTLE-MEN.
LOOKS CAN DECEIVE. ALL OF YOU MIGHT WANT TO TAKE NOTE OF THAT. ♡
skree-eet
RIGHT THEN. LOGI-STICS.
?
WE ARE ON AN ISLAND.
THE ENTIRE ISLAND IS YOUR ARENA. THERE ARE NO "OUT OF BOUNDS." NO SAFE ZONES. ♡
"X" INDICATES YOUR CURRENT LOCATION. THE SCHOOL.

I WILL BE ON THE SCHOOL PREMISES THROUGHOUT THE COMPETITION ...
... OVERSEEING THE TROOPS MONITORING YOUR PROGRESS... OR LACK THEREOF. ♡

......

Tak Tak
THE OCEAN IS NOT AN ESCAPE OPTION. ANYONE FOOLHARDY ENOUGH TO TRY SUCH A COURSE OF ACTION...

......

... WILL BE USED FOR TARGET PRACTICE.
COASTAL PATROL HAS ORDERS TO SHOOT TO KILL.
!

THE ISLAND IS QUITE DESERTED... PRESENT COMPANY EXCEPTED.
COLLATERAL DAMAGE IS NOT AN ISSUE.
SIGH... I WISH YOU COULD HAVE SEEN HOW HONORED THE FORMER RESIDENTS WERE AT THE OPPORTUNITY TO SACRIFICE FOR THE GOOD OF THE PROGRAM. ♡

PATRIOTS ALL. BUT I DIGRESS... PHONE AND POWER LINES ARE DOWN, AS ARE THE WATER MAINS.
STILL, FEEL FREE TO USE ANY STANDING STRUCTURE TO YOUR BEST ADVANTAGE. HIDE IF YOU FEEL YOU MUST... ♡
!

ee-eek
I'D ADVISE AGAINST IT.
YOU'LL BE FLUSHED OUT, SOONER OR LATER, BY THE MORE AMBITIOUS. ATTEND.
!?
NOTE THE GRID.
THE ISLAND HAS BEEN DIVIDED INTO SOMEWHAT EQUAL ZONES.

GIVEN THAT...
AT ANY MOMENT, CERTAIN OF THESE ZONES WILL BE DESIGNATED DANGER ZONES.
skatch skk
D.5
THE DANGER ZONES WILL BE P.A. BROADCAST. "D-5 IS NOW A DANGER ZONE."
YOU WOULD BE WELL ADVISED TO VACATE THAT ZONE WITHIN FIVE MINUTES OF THE ANNOUNCE-MENT.
FAILURE TO DO SO... MOST UN-PLEASANT.
WHICH BRINGS US TO THE COLLARS EACH OF YOU HAVE BEEN FITTED WITH. VERY HIGH-TECH.
VERY EFFECTIVE. AND SHOULD IT RECEIVE THE APPROPRIATE SIGNAL...
ping!
!?
...EXPLOSIVELY LETHAL.

....
FILE THAT UNDER ...
YOU SNOOZE, YOU *LOSE.*

KILL OR ***BE KILLED,*** LITTLE WARRIORS!

EXCELLENT. YOU'LL BE EXITING AT TWO-MINUTE INTERVALS EFFECTIVE IMMEDIATELY.
WE ALL ON THE SAME PAGE? ♡

STARTING WITH...

BOY NUMBER ONE, YOSHIO AKAMATSU.
STEP LIVELY, YOUNG WARRIOR.
!!

Sniff

HERE NOW! WHAT KIND OF EXAMPLE ARE YOU SETTING FOR THE OTHERS?
SEE HOW WE EVEN ALLOW YOU YOUR PERSONAL EFFECTS? ♡
Sniff
Sniff

SNIFF-IFF...
OFF WITH YOU.
GET ON NOW. SHOO.

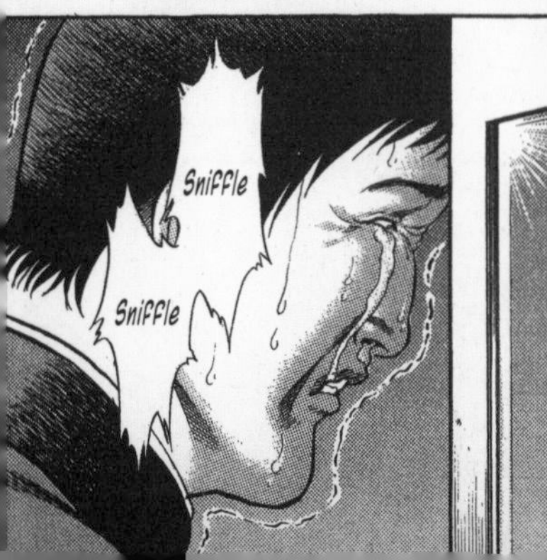
Sniffle
Sniffle

AKAMATSU WOULDN'T HURT A FLY.
C'MON GIGANTOR. ONE MORE SET.
THAT'S... THAT'S DONE ME IN, SHUUYA... HUFF...
THE BIGGEST KID IN THE CLASS... BAWLING LIKE A BABY...
AKAMATSU...
WILL I LOOK THAT SCARED WHEN IT'S MY TURN?

MASTER NANAHARA.
ELVIS IS LEAVING THE BUILDING. ♡

LORD KNOWS MY NIPPLES ARE HARD.
MMM... MUY MACHO... ♡

NORIKO.
?

!
I'LL WAIT FOR YOU OUTSIDE.

......
AH ...
YOUNG LOVE. NEXT UP...
Clat

THIS IS BULLSHIT!
THIS IS SUCH BULLSHIT!
GOTTA THINK THIS THROUGH.
WE GOTTA ALL PULL TOGETHER AND THINK THIS THROUGH.
TOGETHER WE CAN GET THROUGH THIS.
NOBODY'S GONNA BUY INTO THIS PROGRAM SHIT. SHINJI... SHINJI WASN'T BUYING INTO IT. I COULD TELL.
LUCKY FOR YOU I WASN'T. ♡
IF IT WASN'T FOR HIM I'D BE DEAD ALREADY. WE CAN RALLY THE OTHERS.

HE'D BE ALL FOR TURNING THIS AROUND! GOT ALL THE RIGHT MOVES.

......
NOT SO FAST HERE, SHUUYA.

HARD TRUTH IS...
YOU'RE TAKING A LOT ON FAITH.

HOW SURE ARE YOU THAT NOBODY BOUGHT INTO THIS?
HOW MUCH OF YOUR BRAVADO IS JUST WISHFUL THINKING?

HOW WELL DO YOU REALLY KNOW CLASS B?
WELL ENOUGH TO TRUST ANY OF THEM WITH YOUR LIFE? KAWADA?

AND HOW WELL DO YOU REALLY KNOW KURIYAMA?
HE'S NEVER SHOWN HE GIVES A RAT'S ASS OR ANYONE.

HOW WELL DO YOU EALLY KNOW NORIKO?

WHAT ARE YOU THINKING!? THIS IS THE WAY THEY WANT US!
PARANOID... RUNNING SCARED...
GIVE IN TO THAT AND THEY WIN!
OKAY... OKAY...
ONE STEP AT A TIME. FIRST NORIKO...
THEN MIMURA. THEN... THEN PLAY IT AS IT COMES.
SOUNDS LIKE A PLAN!
AND SUGIMURA! HE'S ALREADY OUT THERE.
PROBABLY ALREADY WITH THE OTHERS OUT THERE.
WE'LL STILL HAVE TWENTY-FOUR HOURS.
WE CAN COME UP WITH SOMETHING. I KNOW IT!

......
!
ザザァ…

glint
HELLO ?

IS SOMEONE THERE? I WON'T HURT...

... YOU?
NO. PLEASE, NO...

......
HH!!
MAYUMI?

WHO... WHO COULD ...
DON'T !
AHH!
H- HEH!
H- HEH!
H- HEH!
!!
NN- NGH ...
NO...

A-HEH!
NNNGH ...
A-HEH!
AKAMATSU!!
A-HEH!

Chapter 6: Yoshio Akamatsu

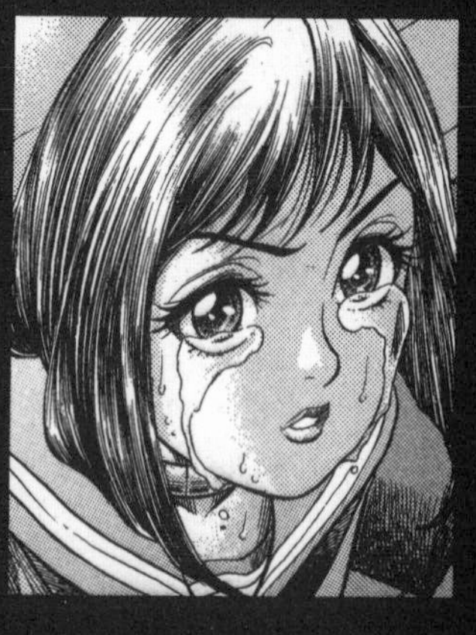

BATTLE ROYALE

AKAMATSU ...
WHAT HAVE YOU DONE? WHY?!

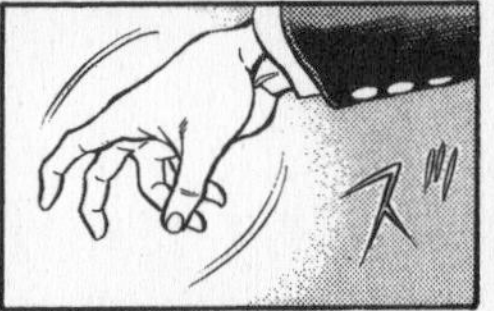

WE DON'T HAVE TO PLAY!
WE CAN BEAT THIS IF WE STICK TOGETHER!

ME!
IT'S ME! IT'S ME!

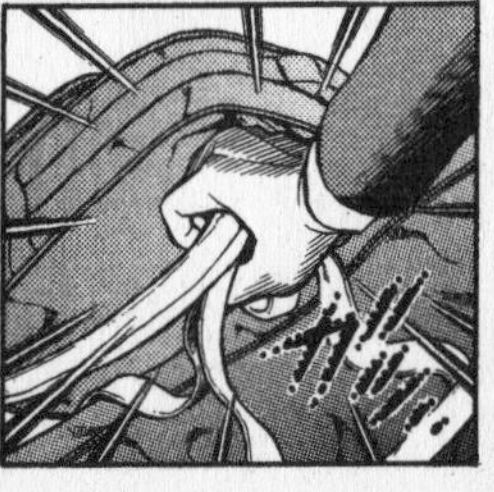

IT'S YOU... I SEE THAT.

NO! IT'S *ME* THEY'LL KILL FIRST! IT'S ME!
I CAN'T... IT'S... I JUST CAN'T...
BECAUSE... BECAUSE I CAN'T! I CAN'T!
I TRY ...
I REALLY, *REALLY* TRY, BUT... BUT...
I JUST... I JUST...
IT'S NOT MY FAULT! WHY IS IT *ALWAYS* MY FAULT?!

WELL, HEY, AKAMATSU. NO PROBLEM.
I'M SURE THE GIRL'S CLASS HAS ROOM FOR ONE MORE.
EVEN THE GIRLS! I DON'T WANT TO BE KILLED BY A GIRL!
A-HEH!
A-HEH!
...FINAL WARNING, BLUBBERBALL. STAY OUT OF MY SIGHT!
UGHF!
SOB ...
I THINK SOMEONE NEEDS DOOFUS BYPASS SURGERY...
TELL ME.
......
AKAMATSU ...

TH- ***THAT'S*** WHY!

THAT'S WHY I DID IT! THAT'S WHY I ***HAVE*** TO KILL FIRST!

IT'S US AGAINST THEM! NOT AGAINST EACH OTHER!
WE PLAY THEIR GAME, WE ALL LOSE! ALL OF US LOSE!!
PROMISE ...
PROMISE YOU WON'T KILL ME.

OR... OR LET THE OTHERS...
......
DON'T LET THEM KILL ME...

......
NO ONE IS GOING TO KILL YOU.
SWEAR ...

HOW'S THIS THEN? I SWEAR THAT NO ONE IS GOING TO KILL ANYONE!
IF! IF WE ALL PUT OUR HEADS TOGETHER AND FIGURE A WAY OUT OF THIS!
GOOD ENOUGH? ♡
WANT A PINKY SWEAR?!
HUH ...
YOU!

YOU WITH YOUR BIG SMILE! JUST LIKE THE OTHERS!
BIG SMILES TILL IT'S TIME TO DUMP ON THE DOOFUS! BIG JOKE!

.....

grind...

!!

.....

SH...SHU?

YOU'RE *NOT* A DOOFUS. NOT TO ME.

AS FOR SMILING... IT'S WHAT *FRIENDS* DO. RIGHT?

TRUST ME ON THIS, AKAMATSU. LIKE I'M TRUSTING YOU *NOT* TO SHOOT ME.

......
Beep Beep
Beep Beep
BEEP-BEEP-BEEP-BEEP-BEEP! COULD YOU POSSIBLY BE MORE ANNOYING?!
TAKE IT OUTSIDE, MAN TITS!
AIEE!
SHU ...!!
HUH?

AKAMATSU. COULDN'T HELP OVERHEARING.
THAT SOUNDS LIKE THE GAME THAT'S BEEN GIVING ME FITS. ANY POINTERS FOR A PAL?
!!
THINK TWICE. NANAHARA GIVES AS GOOD AS HE GETS.
DAMN. FUCKING NANAHARA!
UM... POINTERS? SURE...
WHAT DO YOU--
HERE, LEMME SHOW YOU.
HA! HA-HO!
DIE, FLESH-EATING SCUM!
......
Boop
Beep
SEE? SEE? THEY GOT ME!
NO NO!
JUMP, THEN FIRE! JUMP!

GIVE IT UP, SHUUYA.
!!
THAT'S 'CAUSE YOU DON'T JUMP!
EVERY TIME!!
BLORK

DON'T MIND SHU. GOT A BAD CASE OF THE ROCK AND ROLL PNEUMONIA.
MIMURA MAKES A GOOD POINT...
HMM ...
IT'S A GAME OF FINESSE. TAKES A CERTAIN TOUCH...
THOSE CHIMPANZEE HANDS JUST AREN'T GONNA CUT IT. ♡
......
OOKA.
OOKA.

CAN'T HAVE IT ALL, SHU.
WHAT? NO BOOGIE-WOOGIE FLU?
GIGGLE
GIGGLE

AKAMATSU ...
LOOKS LIKE YOU GOT THE RIGHT TOUCH.
C'MON! SHOW "ALMOST ELVIS" HERE HOW IT'S DONE.

UM ...
SURE.
IT'S REALLY PRETTY EASY.

beep
b'doop
おおーっ!
beep-oop

FRIENDS ...

NANAHARA ...

C'MON DOWN. LET'S GET THINGS GOING. ***OUR*** WAY.
NOW YOU'RE GETTING IT.

YOU GOT IT.

OUR... WAY...

MAYUMI ...

HN...
HN ...
HNGH!
?!

MAYUMI! ***MAYUMI!!*** TOO LATE! TOO LATE FOR ME! MAYUMI IS DEAD!
I'VE ALREADY PLAYED! I'VE PLAYED THE GAME!
WHOSE FRIEND AM I NOW?! I ***KILLED*** HER!
WHO TRUSTS A KILLER? WHOSE ***FRIEND*** AM I NOW?!
THEY DID THIS!
MADE ME GO FIRST!
MADE ME KILL HER! ***DOOFUS! DOOOFUS!!***
AKAMATSU! DON'T DO THIS!

SHUUYA
?

IDIOT GIRL! GET WITH THE PROGRAM!
!!

SHIT!
!!
WHGH
...

NORIKO! YOUR LEG!
!
THE WOUND!
CAN YOU RUN?

I...
YES?
THEN RUN!
!!

THIS WAY! STAY WITH ME!
IT'S HAPPENING!
THE PROGRAM...

THEY'RE PLAYING! I THOUGHT WE COULD... THAT WE WOULD...
GROAN...
WE'VE GOT TO FIND SHELTER! WE'RE SITTING DUCKS OUT HERE!

NORIKO...
PROTECT NORIKO. GET HER TO SAFETY AND... AND...
......
...PROTECT HER...

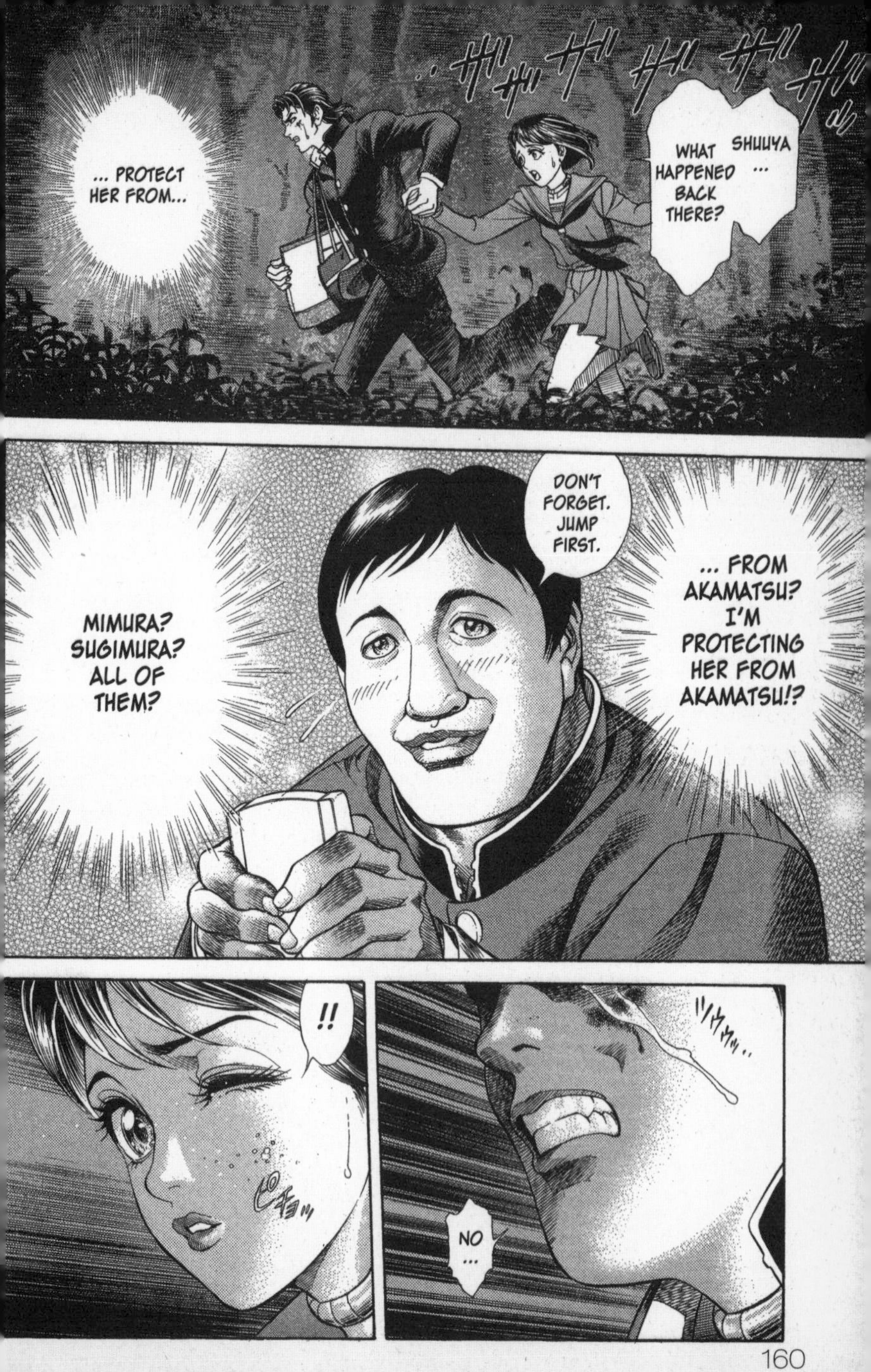

SHUUYA ... WHAT HAPPENED BACK THERE?
... PROTECT HER FROM...
DON'T FORGET. JUMP FIRST.
... FROM AKAMATSU? I'M PROTECTING HER FROM AKAMATSU!?
MIMURA? SUGIMURA? ALL OF THEM?

NO ...

!!

SHUUYA?
PLEASE GOD, NOT FROM ALL OF THEM...
ヒュオオオオ...
MY FRIENDS ...
THESE ARE MY FRIENDS... PLEASE STILL *LET THEM BE* MY FRIENDS...

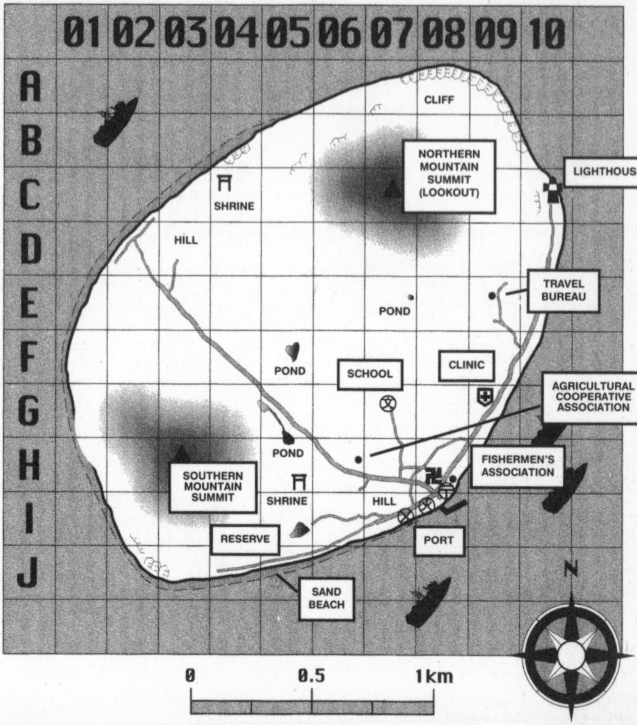

01 02 03 04 05 06 07 08 09 10
A B C D E F G H I J
CLIFF
NORTHERN MOUNTAIN SUMMIT (LOOKOUT)
LIGHTHOUSE
SHRINE
HILL
TRAVEL BUREAU
POND
POND
SCHOOL
CLINIC
AGRICULTURAL COOPERATIVE ASSOCIATION
POND
SOUTHERN MOUNTAIN SUMMIT
SHRINE
HILL
FISHERMEN'S ASSOCIATION
RESERVE
PORT
SAND BEACH
N
0
0.5
1km

Chapter 7: Trust

WE SHOULD... SHOULD BE OKAY... FOR NOW...
HHF ...
HHF ...
CATCH A... A QUICK BREATHER ...
HHF ...
HHF ...
HHF ...
HHF ...

A-
HHF
...
HRN
...

大東亜共和国
大東亜共和国

!

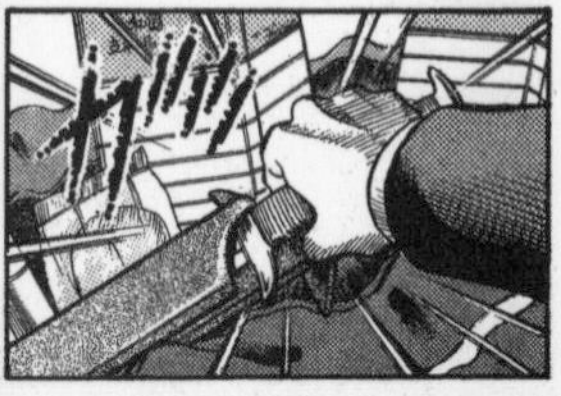

ARMY
KNIFE...
IT'S A
START.

flap

......

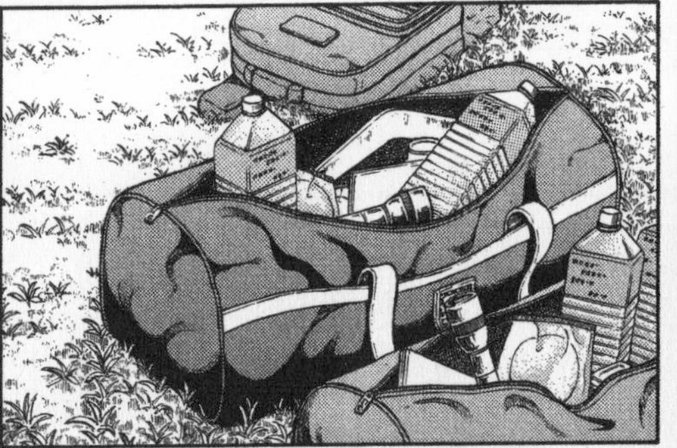

HUH?

A BOOMERANG ?
GIVE ME A FUCKING BREAK!

SORRY ABOUT THIS... PRIORITIES, YOU KNOW?
LET'S HAVE A LOOK AT THAT LEG.

......
EASY. OKAY?

!!

SORRY! I DIDN'T MEAN TO HURT--

OW-OW-OW!

I KNOW.

IT'S... I'M FINE. REALLY.

MAD
LADDE

......
SHIT.
NOT EXACTLY THE CLASS TRIP I EXPECTED.

THIS MIGHT STING A BIT.
PRETTY DECENT FIELD DRESSING, YOU ASK ME.
RIGHT. NOBODY ASKED ME.
sff
IT'S VERY, UM... THANK YOU.

......
YOU'RE WELCOME.

SHU... WHAT HAP--

AKAMATSU *LOST* IT. BIG TIME.
FLIPPED OUT ON FEAR AND ADRENALINE. HE'S PLAYING THE GAME.
FIGURED HE'D BE TARGETED BY THE KIDS WHO USED TO PICK ON HIM. KILL OR BE KILLED, Y'KNOW?
HE WAS PROBABLY RIGHT.
THAT'S THE *HELL* OF IT. HE WAS PROBABLY RIGHT.
HRN...
GOT ME WONDERING WHO MIGHT BE LOOKING TO TAKE ME DOWN.
......
HOW'S THAT FOR YOU? NOT FIVE MINUTES AGO I WAS PREACHING SOLIDARITY.
NOW I'M WONDERING WHICH OF MY "FRIENDS" MIGHT KILL ME.

I MEAN, THAT'S THE IDEA, RIGHT?
KEEP US OFF BALANCE ...
WELL, SURE.

THIS ALL... IT'S HAPPENING SO FAST.
ME TOO.
......

......
KEEPING KIDS ON EDGE, I MEAN. OH HELL, I DON'T KNOW WHAT I MEAN. FEEL FREE TO JUMP IN ANYTIME.
A PANICKED HERD STAMPEDES MORE EASILY. AND THESE PROGRAM GUYS, THEY'VE HAD A LOT OF PRACTICE.

'S OKAY.
I CAN TALK ENOUGH FOR TWO.
ESPECIALLY WHEN I'M NERVOUS, AND I GOTTA ADMIT...
... THIS IS AS NERVOUS AS I'VE *EVER* BEEN.

HUH?

I DON'T THINK I'M A GOOD PERSON. NOT ALWAYS.
......
DO YOU THINK YOU'RE A GOOD PERSON?

NONE OF US IS. NOT EVEN THE GIRLS I HANG OUT WITH.
HOW TRUSTWORTHY DOES THAT MAKE ANY OF US?
I... SEE THINGS ...
......

THINGS THE... THE BAD GIRLS DO.
CYBER-BOM
CLUB
... BLEEDIN' LIKE A STUCK PIG 'N' BAWLIN' LIKE A BABY. HA! ♡
... IT ON OVER HERE 'N' GREASE DADDY'S POLE.

THINGS GOOD GIRLS, SO-CALLED... THINGS THEY TOLERATE.
WOULD I TRUST ANY OF THEM TO DO RIGHT BY ME?
WOULD I DO RIGHT BY THEM... IF I... "FLIPPED OUT ON FEAR AND ADRENALINE"?

SAY ENOUGH OF US DID JOIN FORCES...
WHAT HAPPENS WHEN THE FEAR TAKES HOLD?
AND IT WILL.

TWENTY-FOUR HOURS WITHOUT A KILL AND WE ALL DIE.
WHO CRACKS FIRST? IT'S KILL OR BE KILLED.

ONLY ONE SURVIVES. THAT'S IRREVOCABLE. GIVEN THAT... WHY NOT ME?
......
NOT TOO COLD-BLOODED, NORI.
JEEZ... HEARING IT JUST LAID OUT LIKE THAT...

GUESS I NEEDED TO HEAR IT.
NEEDED TO HEAR SOMEONE ELSE SAY WHAT I COULDN'T BRING MYSELF TO SAY.
IT'S OFFICIAL! TRUST IS DEAD!
I TRUST YOU.
ME?!
HOW CAN YOU ...
?!

TRUST ME?!
YOU DON'T EVEN KNOW ME!
......
I KNOW ENOUGH.

THIS IS A FACE YOU CAN TRUST?
HOW DO YOU KNOW I'M NOT JUST WAITING FOR YOU TO FALL ASLEEP?
HOW DO YOU KNOW I DIDN'T BRING YOU OUT HERE TO DISPOSE OF YOU IN PRIVATE?!

I KNEW YOU WOULDN'T ...

THAT YOU'RE NOT... *THAT* KIND OF BOY.

I SEE YOU AT SCHOOL... WITH YOUR FRIENDS. SO MUCH FUN TO BE WITH...
I'VE SEEN YOU DO THINGS FOR THEM WITH *NOTHING* IN IT FOR YOU.

......
ME.
YOU WATCH... ME?
UH-HUH.

ME.
YOU WATCH ME.
ONE OF THE PRETTIEST GIRLS IN SCHOOL...
AND I NEVER NOTICED? DUH!

......
......

PRETTIEST ?!
!

PRETTIEST?
YOU THINK I'M ONE OF THE PRETTIEST GIRLS?

OH! LISTEN TO ME!
OUR FRIENDS ARE DYING AND... AND HERE I AM CARRYING ON ABOUT...
!

... FOUND A GIRL I KINDA LIKE.
ME TOO, YOSHI...
NOT GOOD.

TELL YOU WHAT. ONCE WE'RE SAFELY OFF THIS ISLAND...
WE'LL CONTINUE THIS CONVERSATION. SEE WHERE IT LEADS.

YOU MUST THINK I'M SO...
OFF THE ISLAND?

YEAH. I'VE THOUGHT IT THROUGH...
...AND OPTED FOR "HOPE."

OPTED? HOPE?
ARE WE BACK TO TRUSTING AGAIN?
I WOULDN'T GO THAT FAR.
BUT I'M WILLING TO TAKE A CHANCE ON BELIEVING THERE HAS TO BE A WAY.
ALL I NEED IS SOMEONE TO BELIEVE WITH ME. WHADDAYA SAY?
EH?

I GUESS IT REALLY COMES DOWN TO FAITH.

FAITH IN YOUR FRIENDS... AND, MOST IMPORTANT, FAITH IN YOURSELF.

......

I HAVE FAITH IN YOU, SHUUYA.

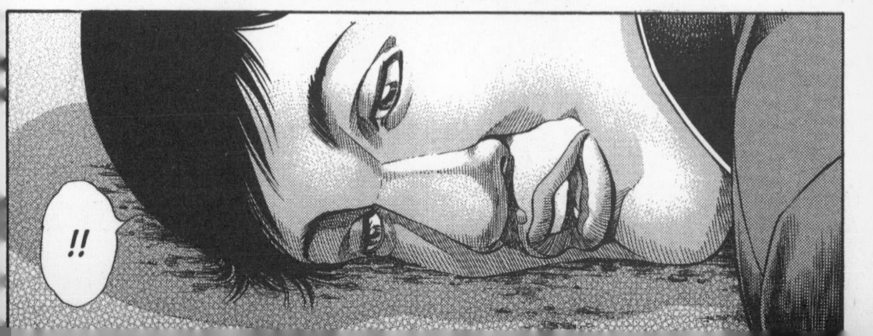

H-HUH!
WHUH ...
SHU ?
SHUUYA ?
BOW ...
MY CROSSBOW !
NEED... NEED MY CROSSBO-
!!
SHUUYA ?

YO ...
YO, MAN TITS...
GOTCHA.
DEAD, BANG.
GOTCHA GOOD.
BAGGED ME A DOOFUS MAN TITICUS... HAW!

THERE FOR THE PICKING, EVERY FUCKING FANTASY I EVER HAD!

GONNA GET ME ALL I CAN GET, MAN TITS. BLOOD 'N' BOO-TAY!

GONNA BE A STAR, DOOFUS, M'MAN. GONNA BE THE MAN!

NINTH GRADE/CLASS - B BOY #16:

KAZUSHI NIIDA

WE CAN'T BE THE ONLY TWO THINKING THIS.

HA!

LIVE AND IN LIVING COLOR! IT'S THE...

... STONE COLD KILLER KAZUSHI NIIDA SHOW! YEEE-HA!

Chapter 8: Mitsuko Souma

ブーンッ‥

CAN'T...

... I JUST...
I CAN'T...

I WON'T
DO IT. I
WON'T!

NINTH GRADE/CLASS B - GIRL #3:

MEGUMI ETOU

PLEASE
...
PLEASE
LET NO
ONE
COME.
PLEASE,
PLEASE
DON'T MAKE
THIS A
DANGER
ZONE...

I CAN'T
GO OUT
THERE...
I
CAN'T...

I WANT
TO GO
HOME...

......
♫

BE
DONE
WITH
IT.
WHY DON'T
YOU JUST
RUB IT RIGHT
ONTO YOUR
THIGHS?

UNLIKE A
CERTAIN
OLDER
SISTER...
I'M STILL
YEARS AWAY
FROM
COTTAGE
CHEESE
THIGHS.

YOU LITTLE BRAT! JUST FOR THAT...
DIBS ON THE STRAWBERRY !
HEY! STOP!
IT'S NOT MY FAULT YOU'VE GROWN OLD AND DUMPY!

SIGH... YOU'D THINK THEY WERE SWORN ENEMIES.
THEY'RE SISTERS. CLOSE ENOUGH.
BUT THE STRAWBERRY'S THE BEST PART!
♪

THEY GROW OLD SO FAST. LITTLE MEGUMI OFF ON HER FIRST OVERNIGHT TRIP TOMORROW...
HM?
NOT SO LITTLE. DID YOU GIVE HER THE CELL?

RIGHT HERE.
I KNOW IT'S PROBABLY "UNCOOL," BUT...

...YOU CALL IF YOU NEED US...

THE CELL PHONE!
I'VE GOT A CELL PHONE!

IT'S STILL HERE!
THEY DIDN'T TAKE IT!

PHONE LINES ARE DOWN... THAT'S WHAT THEY SAID...
DID THEY SCREEN FOR CELL PHONES? DON'T THINK SO!

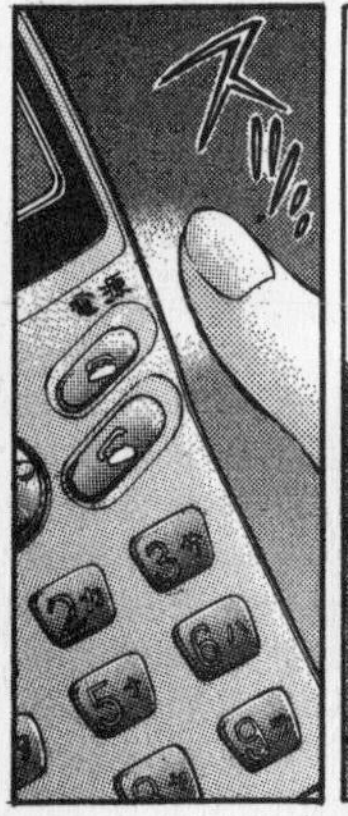

......

HOME
!!

A SIGNAL!

THANKYOU THANKYOU THANKYOU ...
COOLEST EVER, MOM. COOLEST EVER.

IT CON-NECTED! ♡
......
klik

brrt ...
brrt ...
PICK UP... PICK UP... PICK UP...

klik
HELLO?
!!

DAD? DADDY?
THANK YOU... OH, THANK YOU, THANK YOU...
DADDY, IT'S ME! MEGUMI!
THEY TOOK US, DADDY! THEY TOOK ALL OF US!
DADDY WILL MAKE IT ALL RIGHT...
DADDY WILL EXPLAIN TO THEM... MAKE IT RIGHT...
YOU CAN FIX IT, RIGHT?
ALL RIGHT... EVERY-THING'S GOING TO BE...
THEN... THEN I CAN COME... COME... THEN I CAN...

MMMM... WHAT ARE YOU WEARING, YOUNG MUFFIN? DADDY ***MISSES*** HIS PEEK OF PINK... YES, HE DOES. ♡ ♡

YOUR TURN, YOUNG MISSY. TELL ME SOMETHING I CAN MASTURBATE TO, HMMMM? ♡ ♡

HNG!

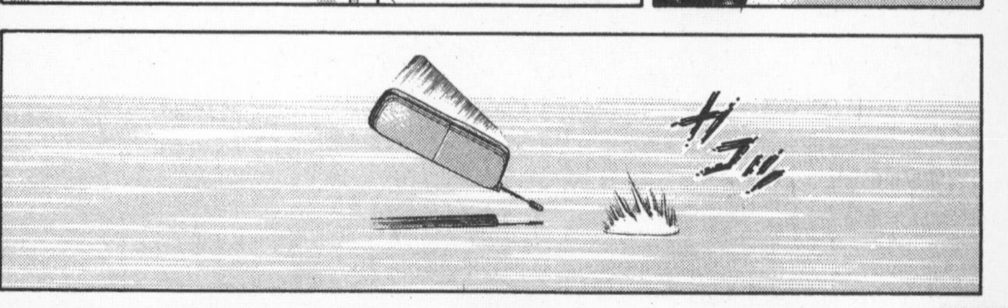

GAHH!
IZZUMS DADDY'S WIDDLE GIRL?

HIH ...
HIH ...

HIH ...

NO... NO...
NO... NO...
A-HIH...

!!

WHO...
NO! STAY AWAY! STAY AWAY!

......

click!

!!
THEY TOLD SOMEONE !
chk

......
TOLD ...
TOLD SOMEONE WHERE I AM...
TOO SMALL... THEY LIED...
THEY SAID GIRLS WOULD GET... WOULD GET GUNS... BETTER STUFF...

HUH!

!

SKIRT... A GIRL... THANK GOD...
WHO? PRETTY LEGS... WHO DO I KNOW...
PRETTY LEGS... PRETTY LEGS... WHO?

MIZUHO!

NO...
MIZUHO... MIZUHO SCRAPED HER KNEE IN GYM...
KAORI HAS PRETTY LEGS... PLEASE BE KAORI...

SIGH...
EMPTY. NO ONE HOME... THANK GOD.
!!
MITSUKO!

MITSUKO SOUMA!
HARD-CORE SOUMA! SHE... SHE'S CRAZY!
CRAZY AND... AND HERE! WITH ME! ALONE!
SHE CUT A BOY... HE HAD TO... HAD TO... THIRTEEN STITCHES!
......
I CAN'T FIGHT HER! SHE CUT A BOY!
SHE'S CRAZY!
NOT ME...
TOO SMALL!
WHAT IF SHE HAS A GUN? OH, PLEASE NOT ME!

!!

WHAT'S THIS?!

NNGH !

NOT ME... NOT MEEEE ...

......
WHO... WHO'S THERE?

PLEASE... I DON'T... WANT TO... IS ANYBODY HERE?
NN-NNNGH-GHH...

NO!!

......
MEGUMI...
TH-THANK GOD...
I... I'VE BEEN RUNNING EVER SINCE THEY... I'M SO GLAD IT'S YOU!
I CAN'T DO THIS.
MITSUKO?

WE CAN... WE CAN HIDE. TOGETHER.
PLEASE ...
LOOK... I DON'T HAVE A WEAPON.
I... I NEED SOMEONE I CAN...
......
PLEASE ...
SEE? NO WEAPON. I NEED **SOMEONE** TO TRUST... TO TRUST ME...

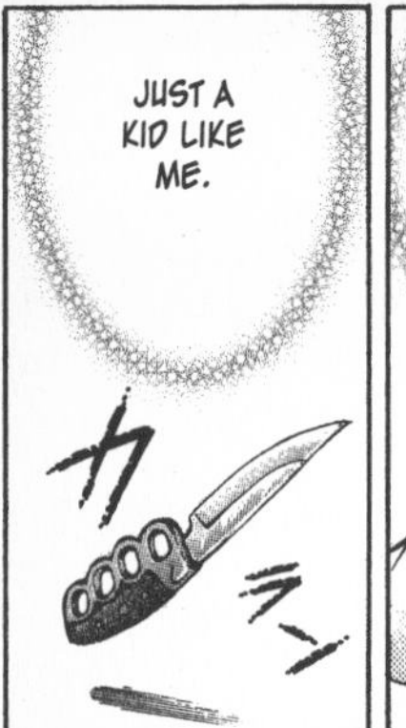

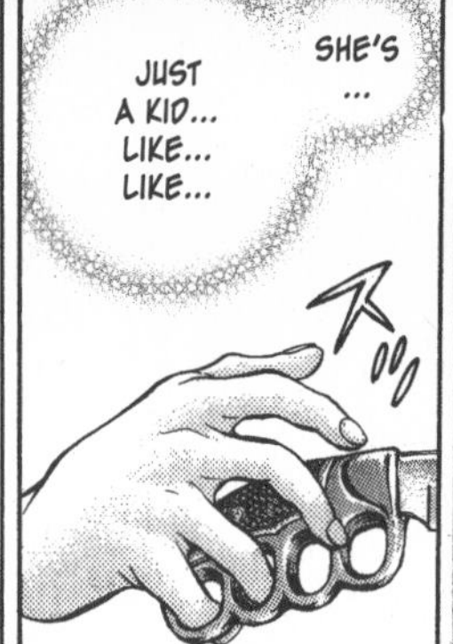

MY SISTER... HER ***REPUTATION*** WAS... BUT SHE DIDN'T DO ANYTHING... MITSUKO...

FRIENDS ?

......

FOR-REAL FRIENDS, MITSUKO. I PROMISE!

FOR-REAL FRIENDS? I'VE NEVER HAD A FOR-REAL FRIEND!

OMIGOD!
MEGUMI!?
WHEN I THINK...
I WAS... WAS...
I WAS SO SCARED AND... AND I THOUGHT...
I THOUGHT YOU WERE COMING TO... TO GET ME...
TO KILL ME. I... I THOUGHT YOU WERE...
I THOUGHT YOU WERE PLAYING THE GAME.
I THINK... I THINK A LOT OF THEM...
I THINK A LOT OF THEM WILL... PLAY THE GAME. A LOT.
I KNOW.. ♡
A LOT OF THEM WILL PLAY...
MITSUKO... JUST LIKE MY SISTER... BAD REPUTATION, GOOD GIRL... PEOPLE CAN BE SO MEAN...
NOT ALONE... I'M NOT ALONE ANYMORE... FOR-REAL FRIENDS... FOR RE--

SURPRISE. ♡

GLK...
HK...

YOU CALLED IT RIGHT, MEGUMI. A LOT OF US ***WILL*** PLAY...
... AND PLAY TO ***WIN.*** NO SENSE PLAYING OTHERWISE, *HMM?*

OH... AND RED? MOST DEFINITELY **NOT** YOUR COLOR. ♡

DO ME PROUD, ***LITTLE WARRIORS.*** DO ME PROUD. ♡

TO BE CONTINUED...

THE PROGRAM: UPDATE

PROGRAM CONDITIONS:
All members of the class must kill each other until one survivor remains • All students are supplied with a ration of food, a map of the island and a weapon • All students will wear an explosive bomb collar which also monitors life signs • Students are free to move about the island but must stay out of designated danger zones that will frequently change locations • If there is more than one survivor at the end of the game, the remaining bomb collars will be detonated.

CHAPTER 7: Shuuya and Noriko rest.

01 02 03 04 05 06 07 08 09 10
A B C D E F G H I J
SCHOOL GROUNDS: PERMANENT DANGER ZONE
SHUUYA'S ROUTE
N
0 0.5 1km

CHAPTER 8: Mitsuko Souma kills Megumi Etou.

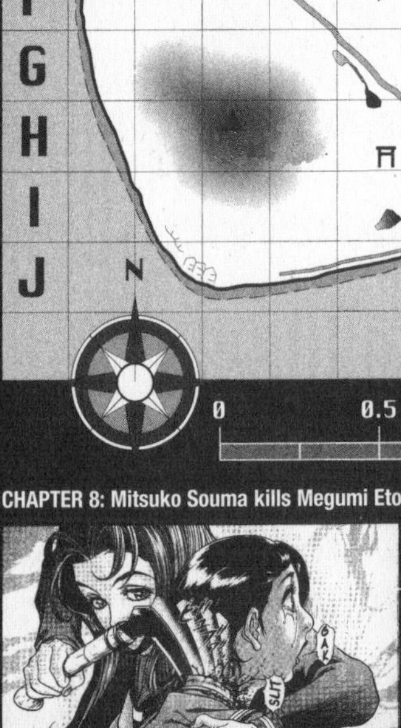

CHAPTER 2: Yoshitoki is shot.

BATTLE ROYALE

KOUSHUN TAKAMI & MASAYUKI TAGUCHI

IN THE NEXT VOLUME OF BATTLE ROYALE:

The demented Mr. Kamon has kicked off the program with more than a few "bangs," and it looks like he's going to get his share of sick kicks now that the carnage has started. While Shuuya reels from this nightmare, he continues his search for friends he can trust. But will his hopes to form an alliance to defeat "The Program" be dashed by the deception and manipulation of those who wish to win the game?

TOKYOPOP®

PRIEST

THE QUICK & THE UNDEAD
IN ONE MACABRE MANGA.
AVAILABLE NOW

www.TOKYOPOP.com

PRIEST © MIN-WOO HYUNG. TOKYOPOP is a registered trademark of Mixx Entertainment Inc.

SAMURAI DEEPER KYO

BY: AKIMINE KAMIJYO

100% AUTHENTIC MANGA

TOKYOPOP

The Action-Packed Samurai Drama that Spawned the Hit Anime!

Slice the surface

to find the assassin within...

SAMURAI DEEPER KYO AVAILABLE AT YOUR FAVORITE BOOK & COMIC STORES NOW!

OT OLDER TEEN AGE 16+

© 1999 Akimine Kamijyo. All rights reserved. First published in Japan in 1999 by Kodansha LTD., Tokyo. English translation rights in the United States of America and Canada arranged by Kodansha LTD. English text © 2003 Mixx Entertainment, Inc. TOKYOPOP is a registered trademark of Mixx Entertainment, Inc. All rights reserved.

www.TOKYOPOP.com

TOKYOPOP®

COWBOY BEBOP

shooting star

Story & Art by:
Cain Kuga

Original Concept by:
Hajime Yatate
©Sunrise

100% AUTHENTIC MANGA

NAMED TO THE N.Y. PUBLIC LIBRARY'S Books FOR THE Teen Age 2003 List

MORE SPIKE
MORE JET
MORE COWBOY BEBOP

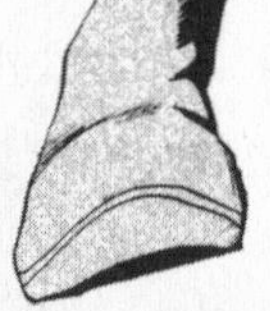

Also Available:
Cowboy Bebop Volumes 1, 2, 3 & Boxed Set
Cowboy Bebop Anime Guides
Volumes 1-6 in stores now! Collect them all!!

T TEEN AGE 13+

www.TOKYOPOP.com

©Yutaka NANTEN ©Hajime YATATE ©Shinichirou WATANABE ©SUNRISE. First published in Japan by KADOKAWA SHOTEN PUBLISHING CO., LTD., Tokyo. English translation rights arranged with KADOKAWA SHOTEN PUBLISHING CO., LTD., Tokyo. through TUTTLE-MORI AGENCY, INC., Tokyo. TOKYOPOP is a registered trademark of Mixx Entertainment, Inc. All rights reserved.

STOP!

This is the back of the book. You wouldn't want to spoil a great ending!

This book is printed "manga-style," in the authentic Japanese right-to-left format. Since none of the artwork has been flipped or altered, readers get to experience the story just as the creator intended. You've been asking for it, so TOKYOPOP® delivered: authentic, hot-off-the-press, and far more fun!

DIRECTIONS

If this is your first time reading manga-style, here's a quick guide to help you understand how it works.

It's easy... just start in the top right panel and follow the numbers. Have fun, and look for more 100% authentic manga from TOKYOPOP®!